JDP

D1303686

Helping Our Veterans

CHARITY &
PHILANTHROPY
UNLEASHED

Hickman County Library
120 W. Swan St.
Centerville, TN 37033

Tammy
Gagne

Mitchell Lane
PUBLISHERS
P.O. Box 196
Hockessin, DE 19707

CHARITY & PHILANTHROPY UNLEASHED

Conquering Disease
Emergency Aid
Environmental Protection
Helping Children with Life-Threatening Medical Issues
Helping Our Veterans
Preserving Human Rights Around the World
The Quest to End World Hunger
Support for Education

Printing 1   2   3   4   5   6   7   8   9

**Library of Congress
Cataloging-in-Publication Data**

Gagne, Tammy.
  Helping our veterans / by Tammy Gagne.
       pages cm. — (Charity and philanthropy)
  Audience: Grade 4 to 8.
  Includes bibliographical references and index.
  ISBN 978-1-61228-572-6 (library bound)
  1. Veterans—Services for—United States—
Juvenile literature. 2. Veterans—United
States—Social conditions—Juvenile literature.
  3. Veterans—Mental health—United States—
Juvenile literature. I. Title.
  UB357.G24 2014
  362.86'80973—dc23

                                            2014006923

eBook ISBN: 9781612286105

                                                    PBP

Contents

Introduction

Seventeen years had passed since Stephen C. Klink had been a soldier in Vietnam. The Vietnam Veterans Memorial, also known as "the Wall," had been finished for a year. But Klink knew that he had to be ready before making the trip. While still at the motel in Washington, DC, he asked his wife if she would mind staying behind for his very first visit. He needed some space; she understood. He took his sunglasses, forgot his camera, and left for the short walk to the memorial.

When he reached the site, he immediately noticed how quiet all the other visitors were. Some left flowers at the base of the Wall, others traced familiar names with their fingertips, and all seemed to be deep in thought. His mind too was wandering back in time.

"After a volunteer showed me how to locate a name," he recalls, "I searched for and found name after name of those who fought beside me. Seeing their names etched in granite, I was glad I'd thought to bring the sunglasses. Tears stung my eyes. I felt my jaw clench and my stomach sink. For years, I'd hoped that maybe a mistake had been made and that my comrades-in-arms weren't really dead. Now, I couldn't escape the truth any longer—they were dead."[1]

Soon Klink took a step back to take in the bigger picture. When he did, he noticed something familiar about many of those other visitors: Everywhere he looked, he saw men just about his age, wearing sunglasses.

"Standing that afternoon in front of a wall of black granite sealed it for me. I could play no more mind games. My search for closure and peace demanded that I now deal with the facts."[2]

For many returning veterans, whether they have been back for seventeen days or seventeen years, dealing with those facts can be a mighty difficult assignment. Fortunately, numerous organizations and programs exist to help United States vets go on with their lives after giving—and often losing—so much of themselves.

CHAPTER 1

Risking Life and Limb

The Panjwayi District is known as the birthplace of the Taliban. Located in Afghanistan just southwest of Kandahar, this area has been the site of some of the longest and bloodiest fights of the last decade in the region. Most people would find it hard to imagine wishing to be back in this virtual minefield. But that's exactly how Nick Keene felt when his catastrophic injury forced him to go back home just five months after his arrival.

"I wish I could have stayed longer," he shares. "It was hard to think that while my guys were sweating, bleeding in the mud, I'm sitting on a couch doing nothing."[1]

The day had begun with Keene behind the wheel of a Stryker armored combat vehicle. As he drove along, the other members of his unit were scanning the roadside for improvised explosive devices, more commonly known as IEDs. Suddenly, a rocket hit just underneath the vehicle. Before Keene could even realize what had happened, a second strike occurred. This one was a direct hit. It threw him out of his seat and into the side of the vehicle with so much power that it broke his back.

Keene was certain that the blast had blown off his legs, but his eyes insisted they were still there. He would later learn that the damaged nerves had cut off all his feeling. The rocket had done equal damage to the vehicle, which Keene could not move more than a few hundred yards before it gave out. He and the rest of his unit, which included his injured lieutenant, could not get away from the eight able-bodied Taliban members that were quickly moving closer.

One of the Marines' jobs in Afghanistan is to destroy improvised explosive devices, or IEDs, whenever the dangerous weapons are found intact. IEDs have killed or seriously injured a large number of US soldiers. Here, members of Marine Wing Support Squadron 274 destroy such a cache, which was discovered by Marines from Lima Company, Third Battalion, Third Marine Regiment. The weapons were found in an abandoned compound in Southern Shorsurak, Helmand province, during Operation New Dawn in 2010.

The twenty-three-year-old managed to wedge himself into a hole in the vehicle just close enough to one of its guns. His arms and hands were still working, so he relied on them to protect his fellow soldiers. Keene's finger didn't leave the trigger until he had fired all 2,800 rounds. For his actions that day, he would receive a Purple Heart—and a one-way ticket home.

The vertebrae in Keene's back were so badly damaged that it took months for him to find out what would happen to his legs. Doctors eventually decided that they didn't need to amputate them. Even then, however, life outside a wheelchair seemed an unlikely possibility. That same spirit that helped him hang on when his unit in Afghanistan needed him kicked in once again. Keene endured months of painful physical therapy so he could get back on his feet, literally. Although he will always need a cane, he can now walk once again.

Keene has mixed feelings about being declared medically unfit for duty. "I could have appealed it," he notes, "but I just can't do my job anymore. I know that."[2]

When asked about her son's actions in the attack that ended his military career, Brenda Keene says she isn't at all surprised. "That's just the way he is. If he didn't do what he did, who knows how many would have died," she shares proudly.[3]

But as Keene makes the transition from soldier to wounded veteran, one thing is clear: His life will never be the same. The frayed nerves that are still intact are at risk of being severed during any of the numerous surgeries that lie ahead of him. If this should happen, Keene could become permanently paralyzed.

Brenda admits, "It's going to make a big impact on his life and has already."[4]

Like Keene, Army Sergeant First Class Dale Smith knows what it's like to return from combat with a disabling injury. While stationed in Afghanistan in 2011, Smith was shot in the head

Iraqi Freedom veteran Charles Matthew Warren is seen here exercising at the Uptown Division of the Department of Veterans Affairs Medical Center in Augusta, Georgia. The facility can provide medical rehabilitation for up to forty patients at one time.

during an attack. Although he is lucky to be alive, the wound robbed him of his eyesight, possibly permanently.

Like Keene, Smith received a Purple Heart shortly after his injury. Upon returning home to Colorado, he was also presented with the Bronze Star with Valor. He brought his own personal cheering section to the ceremony. His wife Lindsey; daughter Cadence and son Sage; parents Dale Sr. and Cindy Smith; and brother and sister-in-law Raymond and Cassie Smith all attended the event.

"I'm not sure if there was a dry eye in the gymnasium when Cadence was lifted up by an army officer so she could re-pin his Purple Heart as he stood tall and strong amongst the troops," recalls Cassie. "I know our family was deeply moved by the ceremony in its entirety."[5]

Following the injury, Smith knew that his life was going to change. But he hasn't let it change who he is. "He is exactly like he was pre-injury," Cassie shares. "He makes jokes, he remembers all sorts of things that happened in his childhood."[6] Those memories are important signs that Smith's long-term memory is coming back after dealing with some memory loss as a result of the gunshot wound.

His family members also understand that things won't always be easy. But they are positive and supportive. "It's a little bit of an adjustment," Cassie says honestly, "but nothing we can't get through."[7]

A higher percentage of veterans are returning from combat with disabling injuries and mental health conditions like post-traumatic stress disorder (PTSD) than ever before. Experts say that part of the reason is how far technology has come in recent decades. Both military armor and rescue operations are far better than they were before. This means that fewer injured soldiers are dying and more are coming home. But those who are coming home often need some help dealing with their issues.

Judi Cheary is the spokeswoman for the Veterans Affairs Medical Center in San Francisco, California. As she explains, "The equipment is better and the medical care is better, so they're surviving injuries that soldiers in other conflicts would have never survived. And we've increased staff, created a bunch of new programs and are actively doing outreach for these young vets to come to us, but unfortunately most of them don't."[8]

Many times, military experience leaves veterans with a belief that they must tough it out on their own. A study by Rand, a nonprofit research group, found that 70 percent of veterans who need help do not ask for it from either the military or Veterans Affairs. Unless these men and women reach out to organizations that can help, nothing can be done.

Cheary stresses, "We want them to know we're here and our doors are open."[9]

The Lt. Dan Band

Gary Sinise played Lieutenant Dan Taylor, a wounded veteran, in the 1994 movie *Forrest Gump*. A skilled musician as well as a talented actor, Sinise plays in a group called the Lt. Dan Band. He named it in honor of the role that earned him an Academy Award nomination. In 2004, Sinise's band began touring with the United Service Organizations. Known better as simply the USO, the organization provides programs, services, and live entertainment for United States soldiers who are stationed overseas.

Sinise plays bass guitar for the band that is made up of a dozen musicians. They play covers from a wide range of pop, rock, and country artists, both new and old. Soldiers lucky enough to attend a concert may hear songs originally performed by Beyoncé, the Zac Brown Band, Lonestar, or Stevie Wonder. "I pick most of the songs," says Sinise, "but band members come up with different ideas. I just want to play a variety. We could go from a Hendrix tune to a Sugarland song and then to an Andrews Sisters tune. It's all over the place."[10]

They typically play between thirty and forty shows each year. While his schedule is definitely a busy one, Sinise knows that he has the easier job compared to the soldiers. "I do spend a lot of weekends on the road. I have to pace myself. It can be pretty busy, but I'm not out in the Afghan desert with seventy pounds on my back, away from my family for a year at a time."[11]

One of Gary Sinise's Lt. Dan Bandmates is Kimo Williams. A Vietnam veteran himself, Williams formed the group with Sinise in 2003. The pair had worked together previously on a Steppenwolf Theatre production of *A Streetcar Named Desire*. The band performed publicly for the first time about a year later on a United Service Organization tour. They have been performing for US troops around the world ever since. Here they are seen during a sound check before a concert at the Fort Bragg, North Carolina, Fairgrounds in 2012.

CHAPTER 2

Down, But Not Out

Army specialist Christian Willard was just twenty-two years old when he experienced one of the most traumatic incidents of his life. On May 29, 2009, the Humvee he was riding in was hit by a grenade in Mosul, Iraq. The next two years of his life would be filled with surgeries and physical therapy to heal the devastating leg wound he suffered that day.

While lying in a hospital bed shortly after the attack, Willard received a gift that made a big impression on him. The black backpack given to him by the Wounded Warriors Project (WWP) was filled with a variety of items. From soap and shampoo to clothing and playing cards, these things would make his hospital stay more comfortable. But what struck Willard the most was the logo on the outside of the bag.

"It was a small thing, but when you see that symbol for the first time, that soldier carrying another soldier, it's cool," remembers Willard. "It feels really good to know that there are people there outside the military who are willing to help you out. It lets you know you're finally home."[1]

The Wounded Warriors Project began in 2003 in Roanoke, Virginia. Three years later the organization moved to Jacksonville, Florida, with a total of fourteen employees. Today the WWP has over two hundred employees in fifteen US offices and one German office. The group works to raise awareness about the problems of injured veterans and get them the aid they need. In addition to the backpack project, the WWP offers numerous other programs and services for veterans—including some that enable vets to help one another. The organization also lobbies on behalf

In 2010, veterans participated in the Wounded Warrior Project Soldier Ride. The three-day event began in San Diego and ended at the Santa Monica Pier in Los Angeles. Thirty participants from the wars in Iraq and Afghanistan rode on adaptive equipment in the journey. According to the Wounded Warrior Project, the annual event helps vets "use cycling and the bonds of service to overcome physical, mental, or emotional wounds."[2]

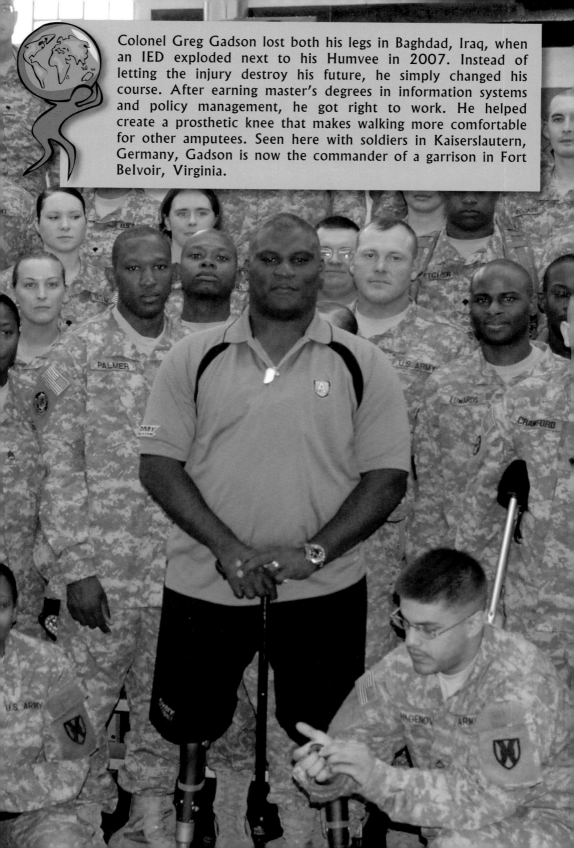

Colonel Greg Gadson lost both his legs in Baghdad, Iraq, when an IED exploded next to his Humvee in 2007. Instead of letting the injury destroy his future, he simply changed his course. After earning master's degrees in information systems and policy management, he got right to work. He helped create a prosthetic knee that makes walking more comfortable for other amputees. Seen here with soldiers in Kaiserslautern, Germany, Gadson is now the commander of a garrison in Fort Belvoir, Virginia.

of service members and their families in Washington, DC. As the WWP slogan states, "The greatest casualty is being forgotten."[3]

The WWP TRACK resource has helped better prepare Willard for life as a civilian. The year-long program gives veterans a head start in getting the training they will need to enter the workforce. He has also met other injured vets and managed to find some time for more leisurely activities like scuba diving with them as a group. "Ever since I got back to Jacksonville my life has pretty much revolved around Wounded Warrior," he shares. "It gives you a second chance."[4]

One of the most inspiring wounded veterans is US Army Colonel Greg Gadson. Google Gadson's name, and you will find information on so many astounding accomplishments that it may take you a while to realize that he lost both his legs in Iraq. In 2007, Gadson was serving as commander of the Second Battalion Thirty-Second Field Artillery unit. While the unit was returning from a memorial service for a fellow regiment, his vehicle was struck by an IED.

The situation didn't look good for the forty-one-year-old soldier. The blast had injured him badly. Fortunately, he had trained his team well. "[They] got tourniquets on my legs and sped me to ground where I could get medevacked out," he remembers.[5] An eighteen-year-old medic who was just a private first class at the time also worked hard to save his life. Gadson says the young soldier yelled at him nonstop, willing him to remain conscious and alive.

The sooner a person reaches a hospital after a serious injury, the greater the odds are that his or her life can be saved. Gadson's team got him there with just minutes to spare. Thankfully, the doctors were able to save him, but it wouldn't be an easy task. In all they gave him seventy pints of blood. Gadson survived the horrific experience, but the doctors had to amputate both his legs.

Faced with a similar situation, many of the bravest and strongest people would have given up. But not Gadson. "At my

In 2012, the US Army honored Fort Belvoir garrison commander Colonel Gregory D. Gadson at the 113th Army vs. Navy football game in Philadelphia.

lowest points, when I wanted to throw in the towel and not live a life associated with losing my legs, I just couldn't quit," he states. "I'd never quit in my life and didn't know how."[6]

Following his recovery, Gadson went back to school. He earned master's degrees in information systems and policy management. He decided to put his education and experience to use by working with scientists on the Power Knee 2. This prosthetic device helps

people who have lost legs from above the knee down walk more easily and safely. Not only had Gadson come back from his own injury, but he was also helping others in similar situations. He donates his time to the US Army Wounded Warrior Program (separate from the Wounded Warrior Project) as well.

Even while he was still recovering, Gadson was already helping others. Following his injury, an old football teammate got in touch with him. This longtime friend was Mike Sullivan, a coach for the New York Giants football team. Sullivan asked Gadson to speak to his players, who were off to a discouraging start for the 2007-2008 season.

Gadson spoke to the team while he was still in a wheelchair. "I talked to them about their gifts as athletes, and the privilege and special opportunity that they have," he recalls. He also spoke to them about the power of a team. "I told them that when we're deployed, we're fighting for our country and our flag and mom and dad and apple pie, but when it comes down to it, those things are the furthest thing from your mind. You're fighting for that guy that is right next to you. Just like my soldiers, who came and fought for me and saved my life."[7]

The talk ended with a standing ovation. Gadson's words appeared to make a difference to the struggling team, as the Giants won their next game the following day with a final score of 24 to 17. And the wins kept coming. The team asked Gadson to serve as honorary co-captain when they played the NFC Championship Game. When they won Super Bowl XLII a few weeks later, the Giants awarded him a Super Bowl ring.

Gadson also got to try something he had never done before: acting. He played a Special Forces Army officer in the 2012 action movie *Battleship*. The role seemed to be a bit of a hint of what was to come for Gadson. Later that year he became the commander of a garrison in Fort Belvoir, Virginia. "I was pretty surprised when I came out on the command list," he admits, "and I'm humbled and honored the Army is allowing me the opportunity to soldier on."[8]

When he speaks about his remarkable recovery, he's positive yet honest. "There are no shortcuts in healing. It's a process. As dramatic as it is physically, it's much more challenging emotionally and intellectually. What I found out is life is not about what we don't have; it's about what we have. I feel so fortunate to be here and have the opportunity to continue serving."[9]

Helping Homeless Veterans

Some veterans come home with an overwhelming feeling of helplessness. No matter how hard they try, they can't seem to put their lives back together after everything they have seen in combat. In many cases the vets are suffering from a condition like Post Traumatic Stress Disorder (PTSD) or depression. A high percentage of these men and women turn to drugs and alcohol to help them deal with their hopeless feelings. Instead of helping, though, this method of coping just makes their problems worse. Substance abuse can cause a person to lose many positive things including their spouse, family members, and job.

To add to the problem, many veterans who choose this route eventually wind up homeless. The Emergency Services and Homeless Coalition in Jacksonville, Florida, works to help local vets who find themselves in this devastating situation. A 2012 survey by the organization showed a strong presence of homeless veterans in the city. Of the 2,861 people without homes in Jacksonville at the time, about 15 percent were veterans.[10] Fortunately, these numbers have gotten the issue some much-needed attention.

Alvin Brown is Jacksonville's mayor. With the help of a grant from the Department of Labor, he helped launch the Homeless Veteran Reintegration Program in the city. Its purpose is to help vets who are already homeless or who are in danger of losing their homes. In just one year, one hundred people had already received job assessments to help get them back to work. Brown states, "If an individual who has defended us and protected us and given us our freedom is now homeless, that is unacceptable. As mayor, my goal is to eradicate homelessness amongst veterans."[11]

Alvin Brown, mayor of Jacksonville, Florida, attends the grand opening ceremony at Naval Hospital Jacksonville. The project took a total of $60 million and five years to complete. The upgrade added six new operating rooms, an underwater treadmill, and a state-of-the-art pharmacy.

CHAPTER 3

The Wounds You Can't See

Returning to life as a civilian isn't always easy. Veterans must move from the structure of their lives as soldiers and the dangers of working in combat to new realities. Life back home is often far less controlled. Where to live, how to support themselves and their families—even what they will do with their free time—is now completely up to these men and women themselves. When compared to combat, life at home is also much less dangerous. But we also must consider the mental toll of combat; new dangers await many soldiers on the home front.

After experiencing war firsthand, many soldiers have a hard time leaving those memories behind them and moving on. The visual images and frightening sounds linger on in the minds of these veterans. Some relive the horrors each night in the form of nightmares. Some suffer from mental illnesses such as depression or PTSD. These conditions can become very serious, especially without treatment.

We hear about the lives lost overseas when we listen to news reports. What we don't hear about as often, though, are the men and women who are becoming victims after they have returned. More veterans have committed suicide after returning from Iraq and Afghanistan than have died in combat there. Some estimates place the numbers at 6,500 suicides each year—18 each day.[1]

Marine Clay Hunt served back-to-back tours of Iraq and Afghanistan. Even after becoming critically wounded in Fullujah, he returned to combat the following year. When he finished his service, Hunt took part in an important campaign. Its purpose was to encourage veterans to reach out if they were considering

President Barack Obama spoke at the Disabled American Veterans National Convention in Orlando, Florida, in 2013. His speech addressed the need to process veterans' claims more quickly and the importance of conducting research into traumatic brain injury and post-traumatic stress disorder.

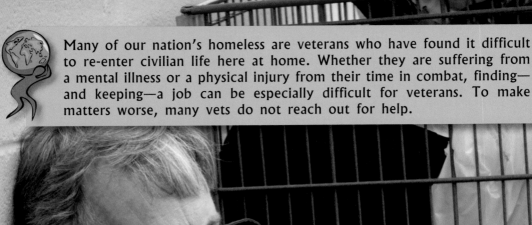

Many of our nation's homeless are veterans who have found it difficult to re-enter civilian life here at home. Whether they are suffering from a mental illness or a physical injury from their time in combat, finding—and keeping—a job can be especially difficult for veterans. To make matters worse, many vets do not reach out for help.

suicide. Sadly, Hunt took his own life in 2011. His best friend pleads, "Let us learn a hard lesson from this, that some of us are still fighting the war, even though we're home and out of uniform."[2]

Dr. James Boehnlein is a psychiatrist and post-traumatic stress specialist at Oregon Health and Science University. He shares that multiple tours often result in brain injuries, but knowledge about this is relatively new. "Blasts caused by explosions can cause injury even if the soldier didn't hit their head on something or black out," he explains. "There's a complex gray area of trauma from blast injury mixed with psychological or emotional injury that can cause headaches, sleep disturbance, and other symptoms of post-traumatic stress. People tend to self-medicate, and drugs and alcohol make the problems worse."[3]

Fred Gusman is a social worker and mental health specialist in Yountville, California. He works as the director of the Pathway Home, a nonprofit residential treatment center for active and retired service members. He describes PTSD this way: "You shut down emotionally except when you're raging with anger. You are hyper-vigilant because you don't know where the enemy is. You look for signs of trouble in the line at Wal-Mart, or when someone crowds you on the freeway, or when there's a sudden noise. They are very, very watchful. This kept them alive in Iraq and Afghanistan, but it becomes a problem when they come home. It's not like a light switch you can turn off or on. I tell the guys they have to play detective, to figure out why they're angry or anxious and unravel it. We give them the tools to realize when they're spinning and need to stop. They learn to modulate their emotions."[4]

Trevor Dallas-Orr is a retired senior chief of the US Navy. He insists, "No movie begins to portray the horror, the shock, the emotional aspect of being there. . . . I lost my family, my job, my home, my identity. Fred's team opened me up and I started to realize, 'Hey, this is a good thing.' If it hadn't been for this place, I'd be dead. I would've just melted away."[5]

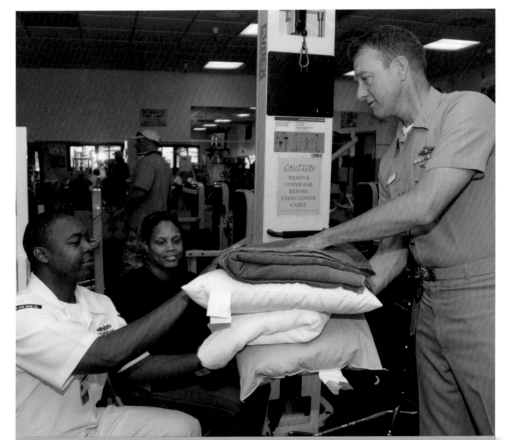

In 2007, Trevor Dallas-Orr (right) welcomes Navy Personnel Specialist First Class William Clincy and his wife, who were temporarily relocated due to a wildfire. Several years later, Fred Gusman of Pathway Home welcomed Dallas-Orr, who suffered from PTSD after he retired from the Navy. The program helped him learn to manage his condition.

Following nearly a year of treatment at Pathway Home, Dallas-Orr returned to his home in Southern California. His PTSD isn't gone, but he has learned how to manage it. He is back in touch with his two sons. He even spoke in front of hundreds of people at a state event called Operation Welcome Home, which honored returning soldiers. He says he never could have done that before he went through Pathway's program.

While talking with Dallas-Orr about how far he has come, Gusman refuses to take the credit. "Well, I always say you guys are doing it yourselves," he reminds him. "It's your courage that pushes you forward. Our joy is seeing you being successful in your own right."[6]

The effects of PTSD can last a long time. Vietnam veteran Bob Dawes still suffers from PTSD, but he also helps others battling the condition. He is now an instructor for Outward Bound, an outdoor education organization that works with a wide range of people, including veterans. Some experts think that the rhythm of many outdoor activities has a soothing effect for PTSD victims. Hiking, running, cycling, and even Nordic skiing may offer veterans dealing with the condition some much-needed stress relief. Dawes also notes that just spending time with other vets who are taking part in an Outward Bound experience can be helpful. He shares, "The most healing occurs while [people are] drinking coffee and hanging out by the river. They realize, 'Hey, I'm not the only one who feels this way.'"[7]

Outward Bound is known for its intense physical and mental demands, and these are still part of the experience for veterans taking part. Dawes explains, "You need to recognize when people need to be pushed and when they need to be supported."[8] Instructors are trained to look for signs of PTSD, so they can help the vets with undiagnosed cases seek treatment.

In one situation Dawes realized a young vet was having a hard time when he couldn't bring himself to trust the rope while rappelling. Matthew Friedman is the executive director of the Department of Veterans Affairs' National Center for PTSD. He says that trouble with trust is common with this condition. "If a vet believes, erroneously or not, that his commanding officer led him into an ambush, that can translate into mistrust of authority."[9]

With a complicated problem like PTSD, the solution isn't going to be simple. Help comes in many different ways—some

Outward Bound organizes outdoor adventures that include activities such as hiking, running, and cycling for a variety of people, including veterans. Here, Staff Sgt. Lindsay Howard is seen leading a group of participants in the "Wonderland of Rocks" in Joshua Tree National Park in southeastern California. Many vets suffering from problems like PTSD find that the rigorous physical activity of Outward Bound programs, as well as the time spent with other veterans, makes them feel better.

bigger than others. Both Dawes and Friedman know that Outward Bound experiences can't cure PTSD, but they both think that they can help tremendously. As Friedman points out, "We all return from an outdoor activity feeling better about ourselves, our world, and our colleagues."[10]

A Head Start on Healing

Military members in charge of deployments are considering making some changes in an attempt to reduce the cases of PTSD among soldiers. They may be starting by offering more off-duty time at home to soldiers who do more than one overseas tour. Many veterans who suffer from the condition have served two or more deployments with hardly any time at all in between.

Gresford Lewishall is the vice president of The Stay Strong Nation, a nonprofit organization working to help veterans cope with the condition. He explains, "We are beginning to see the military and research worlds come together in a true effort to study post-traumatic stress, its effects, and different treatments that can help our troops live better lives."[11]

Research has shown that prevention starts with stress management. By giving returning troops more time to spend with family and friends, those soldiers can better deal with the stress they are experiencing. Having a means of releasing some of this tension before heading back into a combat situation could play a key role in keeping the soldier from developing PTSD down the road.

Experts compare sending a soldier with PTSD back into combat to putting a football player with a concussion back in a game. In both cases the problem is bound to get worse if it isn't treated properly and promptly. And in many cases it could be deadly. Ideally, the military wants to prevent as many cases of PTSD as it can. Time will tell whether providing this additional time off can stop the problem from developing in the first place. For many soldiers one of the best parts of returning home is seeing their family members again.

Researchers believe that giving soldiers more time at home with their families in between tours might prevent future cases of PTSD.

CHAPTER 4

Starting Over

Our veterans fight for the very freedoms that we all enjoy—and often take for granted. Simply put, they are heroes. But when they return to the United States after serving the country they love, many vets are treated like second-class citizens. Opinions about whether the United States should be involved in various conflicts around the world often have a damaging effect. Sometimes they even influence the ways that some people treat these brave men and women who have put their lives on the line to protect our very right to disagree with our government's decisions.

Even people who support the troops during times of active duty may forget about them once they return home. No one knows this better than Nick Colgin, a retired specialist from the US Army. While overseas, Colgin did some amazing things including saving forty-two Afghanis from a flooding river and performing combat care on numerous individuals. He even received the prestigious Bronze Star when he came home. But still he couldn't find employment.

"When I got back, the one thing I wanted to do was go out and get a job," says Colgin. "I wanted to go right into the career field. I wasn't asking to be a CEO of a corporation. I was just asking to do what I did overseas. I wanted to be an asset to my community, pay taxes and just—I wanted to be a staple within my community and not a burden on it."[1]

Like so many other returning soldiers, Colgin never expected to find himself in this difficult position. Thinking back to when he entered the military, he shares, "I remember going . . . through all my medical training, and friends and family, people within

Nick Colgin spoke at the Iraq and Afghanistan Veterans of America Fifth Annual Heroes Gala in New York City in 2011. The retired specialist for the US Army did not realize how hard it would be to find work after returning home from his service. He had left the army with many valuable skills that he had learned during his time with the Army. But still, no one would hire him to put that training to use at home.

the military, they were always like, 'oh, you're going to be set when you get out with a job. You're going to be set for life. It's such a smart thing that you're doing,' everything like that. And it lures you into a false sense of confidence. You don't realize that when you get out, the civilian world, it doesn't care what you did in the military, and it really should."[2]

Colgin is careful to point out that he doesn't expect to be treated differently either for better or for worse. "I don't think because of my service I should be given an edge. We're not looking for handouts. We're just looking for an opportunity, to give us a fair shot. . . . Imagine if you took a civilian and put them in Afghanistan tomorrow. They would have a hard time transitioning. And someone like myself and all the other veterans out there, we basically go right into the military out of high school in a lot of cases. So we don't really grow up on the civilian side. . . . We're working at it, it's just we can't do it all by ourselves. We need a little bit of help."[3]

Joseph Jennings served as a cavalry scout in the United States Army until he was released on a medical discharge two years into his tour of Iraq. Jennings had seen some horrible things shortly after completing his Advanced Individual Training in 2003. "I saw the reality of war two weeks into my deployment . . . I saw my best friend blown up," he remembers.[4] Jennings was just nineteen years old at the time.

Suffering from post-traumatic stress disorder, Jennings found everyday life to be enormously difficult upon his return home to Minnesota. His part in the war may have been over, but the battles were raging on in his mind. "For three years it was non-stop on alert, like I was on a patrol or a convoy," he shares. "I honestly thought for a while that there were snipers out on the streets in my hometown."[5]

Things started getting better when Jennings turned to the Veterans Affairs system for help. He managed to set some goals and start working on his college education. He was on a good path, but it wasn't an easy one. Jennings's PTSD made it hard for

Derek Blumke (left) created Student Veterans of America (SVA) in 2007. The organization hosted the Campaign for a New GI Bill the following year. President of SVA, Blumke is seen here at the event in Los Angeles, California, with actor Tony Shalhoub.

him to pay attention in class. He also felt out of place amongst all the younger students. Their experiences had been very different from his—or so he thought.

Jennings soon realized that he wasn't the only veteran on campus. Wanting to connect with the others, he co-founded a veterans' club at Minneapolis Community and Technical College. The group later became part of the national organization Student Veterans of America (SVA), which helps vets succeed in both school and civilian society. "I think the greatest sense of loss I had when I left the military was losing my brothers," says Jennings, "but now I've found new brothers. . . . It gives you a sense of not being alone."[6]

SVA president Derek Blumke created the organization in 2007 when he started college after six years in the US Air Force. His single club went national the following year. It now has more than seven hundred chapters across the United States. Each one operates a little differently. Most commonly, the clubs hold meetings where veterans can gather to talk about their experiences, past and present. They also plan community service events to help others.

Suzette McGraw spent twelve years in the US Army before she rejoined civilian life and started college. She is now the SVA University of Michigan state director for three college campuses. She recalls having worries similar to the ones Jennings had when he re-entered a classroom. Did she belong? Was it too late? "We're very self-sufficient people and so it's difficult for us to ask for help—that's the way we've been trained."[7]

For those who reach out, however, the rewards can be numerous. Completing post-secondary education increases a person's chances of getting a higher-paying job. Latoya Hill is the assistant dean of students at the University of Texas at Austin. She has seen an increase in the number of vets going back to school. "Veterans are coming back and using their educational benefits in droves," she states.[8]

Texas A&M University has also seen a spike in enrolled vets in recent years. The school even added a Veterans Service Office in 2009, as well as a Student Veterans Advisory Council in 2011. The council includes a student representative from each of the Texas A&M System's eleven universities and the Health Science Center. Together the students work to create a better college experience for the veterans on campus.

Andrew Wheeler, the group's chairperson, is a student of the Mays Business School at the College Station campus. He says he would like to see a fast track for veterans interested in registering for classes. "From a big picture standpoint, we want these people back in society, working and contributing to the economy," he says. "They're good people. They've earned it."[9]

The High Cost of Education

One of the biggest barriers between veterans and higher education is something called residency. Current legislation pays for in-state tuition for veterans who have served since the September 11 attacks. But many states require that a student live in that particular state for a certain amount of time before he or she qualifies for in-state tuition rates. Students who reside in other states have to pay higher amounts for tuition. Since military members must move wherever they get stationed, they may not have stayed anywhere long enough to receive the in-state price.

Although it is easy to blame the state universities for this problem, the responsibility actually rests with each state's education department guidelines. All state schools must follow these rules in setting up tuition rates. Fortunately, these rules are beginning to change. So far nine states have passed laws that make it possible for vets to get the in-state rate regardless of length of residency.[10]

This change isn't just good for the veterans. It's also good for the states themselves. When vets decide to spend their education benefits in a specific state, they also spend money on other things in the area. While going to school, after all, the veterans will need a place to live, food to eat, and things to do with their free time. All this spending helps individual state economies.

By being able to get an education without out-of-pocket tuition expenses, the vets leave school in a better position. A veteran who has earned a bachelor's or master's degree, for example, has a much better chance at finding a high-paying job than one who has only earned an associate's degree.

More and more veterans are enrolling in college upon returning home from their service.

CHAPTER 5
You're Hired!

For most returning veterans, creating a happy, productive life as a civilian begins with finding employment. In today's economy, though, finding a good job can be a difficult task for anyone. It is an especially tough undertaking for someone who has had bigger things to worry about than polishing their resume in recent years. Senator Patty Murray from the state of Washington understands this problem. "Our veterans have the drive, discipline, and self confidence to succeed in any workplace," she points out. "But for too long at the end of their career we've patted them on the back for their service and pushed them out into the job market alone."[1]

One American company that is actively seeking to employ veterans is Boeing. The world's largest aerospace company and the leading manufacturer of commercial jetliners and military aircraft launched an online military skills translator in 2011. This program was designed to help vets see how their military experience can be put to use at Boeing.

Former Marine Daniel Barrow did just that. He had been out of the military for four years when he heard about a three-month training program at the Washington Aerospace Training and Research Center. Barrow completed the online portion of the training while still living in Las Vegas, Nevada, where he was working in hotel management. Two weeks after he finished his training, Boeing offered Barrow a job on its 767 assembly line. He and his family moved to Everett, Washington, so he could accept the new position.

In 2011, Boeing won a contract with the United States Air Force to build twin-engine tankers, which are based on Boeing's

US Senator Patty Murray has spoken out about the problems veterans are facing when trying to find jobs after they return home from service. She thinks it is important that our country doesn't abandon these former soldiers at this crucial time.

767 airliners. For Barrow, the contract sealed the deal. "That was one of the things that drew me to Boeing—the prospect of building planes for the military. Anything that's going to help our servicemen and women, that's a good thing."[2]

Most veterans already have valuable skills that they learned in the military. The problem is that they often can't get jobs performing these same tasks back at home. Many states require that people performing certain jobs have licenses or other certifications, and they won't accept military training in place of those official documents.

Montana Senator Elsie Arntzen wants to solve this problem. She points out that her state's unemployment rate for post-9/11 vets is 17.5 percent—more than triple the state average of 5.7 percent. "It is critical that we give recognition for military service and training for state licensing, to help these Montanans transition into jobs in the private workforce," she urges.[3]

Tanya Pullin, a representative from Kentucky, agrees. "I think we have an obligation to find ways to give veterans every opportunity to apply their military experience to academic credit, job certification, or vocation training credits," she says.[4] Pullin, who chairs the House Veterans Military Affairs and Public Safety Committee, is already making progress in this area. In 2013, she sponsored a successful bill that helped vets receive licensing as firefighters and emergency medical technicians.

Alaska Representative Dan Saddler passed legislation on the issue in his state the same year. Most state licensing boards, the University of Alaska, and vocational education facilities in that state must now accept military training and experience when making licensing decisions. As long as a veteran's training and experience relate to a specific degree, both can now be used for granting the vet educational credits. Saddler declares, "Americans in military service receive world-class training, education, and experience during their time in uniform, assets that shouldn't be lost to them or to our communities as they transition to civilian careers."[5]

Tanya Pullin is a representative in the Kentucky legislature. She is also the chairperson for the House Veterans, Military Affairs, and Public Safety Committee. She and many other lawmakers want to make it easier for veterans to get academic credit for what they have already learned through their military training.

Federal lawmakers are also working to make it easier for veterans to transition into jobs that require licensing. A US Department of Defense task force was established in 2012 for this purpose. Working with states and their regulatory agencies, educators, and businesses, the task force's goal is creating criteria for specific jobs in terms of military experience. Bus and truck drivers, emergency medical technicians, paramedics, and licensed practical nurses are among the most common roles that veterans have fulfilled while in the service—and all require some sort of licensing.

Finding a job can be tough enough for veterans whose former roles have a civilian counterpart. But for some veterans, matching their qualifications to a suitable job at home can seem nearly impossible. Anne St. Eloi guides the United Association of Veterans In Piping (VIP) Program. She explains, "Not only are

they trying to find a job in a jobless economy, they often find out the job they did in the military doesn't translate into a civilian job. If they are lucky enough to find a job, they often are underpaid, and their military training undervalued. Plus, in the military, they were taught to think in terms of a team rather than 'I,' and now they must change their whole mind-set to survive and thrive in the corporate world."[6]

That's where the VIP program can help. Vets admitted into the program complete 720 hours of training. The first two weeks focuses entirely on transitioning to life as a civilian. After that the vets then go through sixteen weeks of fast-paced technical training in welding, piping, or heating and ventilation. Once they finish this training, they are ready to begin apprenticeships,

Many veterans find that their military jobs have no civilian counterpart. Wisconsin veterans in this position may find help through a new program created by Wisconsin Army National Guard. Colonel Kenneth Coon is the chief of staff for the Wisconsin Army National Guard. He signed an agreement that paved the way for free training and certifications in the fields of welding, steam fitting, plumbing, and piping.

which last for four years. The veterans who complete their apprenticeships are guaranteed a job, usually making at least $40 per hour, including benefits.

One of the best parts of the VIP program is how the instruction is performed. "The way we train is not too different from how the military trains in that we provide continuous guidance," says St. Eloi. And the support the vets receive is ongoing. "We encourage our students to keep in touch even after the transitional training, which is called Training for Tomorrow, Today!"[7]

Another program that is helping veterans find work is Helmets to Hardhats. The nonprofit organization helps vets find quality careers in the construction industry. Many younger veterans are having an even harder time finding jobs upon returning from

The Helmets to Hardhats program helps veterans by providing them with the training they need to enter the building trades. Jack Anderson spent more than four years in active duty as part of the US Army 82nd Airborne. Now he is a carpenter apprentice. Anderson is seen here, framing a structure.

their service. Helmets to Hardhats offers returning vets a fast-track to employment with certain unions. Aldo Zambetti is the coordinator at the Local 19 training center in Philadelphia, Pennsylvania. "We accept the honorable discharge and say we want that kind of candidate. I am the human resources department," he explains. "I can have the resume and see if someone has HVAC experience or construction experience and put them to work as long as it's available."[8] Those without experience are given the opportunity to learn, and then work as soon as they have the skills necessary for a particular job.

"We've always had a great experience with Helmets to Hardhats apprentices," Zambetti says. "I've not seen one dropout. I've never seen one person fail to graduate to be a journeyperson. I see the Helmets to Hardhats vets in their first five years at their positions, and they are holding higher level jobs, and I think it's because of their military training."[9]

Suiting Up

Serving in the military seems to run in Scott Sokolowski's blood. His grandfather served in the United States Coast Guard, his father served in the US Navy, and he spent six years in the US Air Force himself. It was when he was interviewing a young job candidate in the business world, however, that he was inspired to start the Save-A-Suit Foundation for veterans. When he asked the young veteran why he hadn't worn a suit that day, the vet confided that he couldn't afford to buy one. That one honest answer led to a charity that helps veterans dress for the jobs they want.

The charity collects gently worn or new suits and then gives them to veterans who can put them to good use. It also helps recent college graduates who are trying to enter the job market. Sokolowski shared that one of his biggest donors was former New York Knicks Head Coach Mike D'Antoni. "Before leaving to go coach the Olympics, he invited us to his house and gave us tons of suits, shirts, and ties. And that was really awesome."[10]

Finding employment in the current job market is difficult even for those who can afford to buy a suit. For those who can't afford to look their best, the chances of getting hired are often slim. Jessica Ewud is Save-A-Suit's executive director. She points out, "It's extremely important the way you present yourself in an interview. You have about thirty seconds to give a good first impression."[11]

Los Angeles Lakers coach Mike D'Antoni is among the many supporters of the Save-A-Suit Foundation. The charity helps veterans look their best for job interviews by providing them with business clothing.

WHAT YOU CAN DO TO HELP

Adults aren't the only ones who can help veterans. If you want to get involved, consider some of the ways you can make a difference:

Check out Kids for Our Troops. This division of Homes for Our Troops was created especially for young people who want to help: http://www.kidsforourtroops.org/

Organize a fundraiser at your school to benefit a veterans organization, such as the Wounded Warrior Project.

Many veterans have valuable knowledge about our nation's history. Sharing this knowledge can give a vet a sense of accomplishment and pride. Interview a veteran and write about what you learn. You can even submit your writing to the Library of Congress through the Veterans History Project: http://www.loc.gov/vets/

Volunteer at your local Veterans Administration hospital or nursing home.

When you meet a current service member or veteran, thank that person for his or her service.

CHAPTER NOTES

Introduction
1. Stephen C. Klink, "Sunglasses," in *Chicken Soup for the Veteran's Soul,* eds. Jack Canfield, Mark Victor, and Sidney R. Slagter, (Deerfield Beach, FL: Health Communications, Inc., 2001).
2. Ibid.

Chapter 1: Risking Life and Limb
1. Tim Trainor, *Billings Gazette,* "Heroic Firefight With Taliban Forever Changes Butte Soldier's Life," June 24, 2012.
2. Ibid.
3. Ibid.
4. Ibid.
5. Kevin Wilson, *Clovis News Journal,* "Some Normalcy Returning for Injured Soldier," June 16, 2012.
6. Ibid.
7. Ibid.
8. Kevin Fagan, *San Francisco Chronicle,* "Returning Soldiers Need More Help Sooner," November 30, 2009.
9. Ibid.
10. Robert Abele, *Idaho State Journal,* "Gary Sinise: The Actor-Activist Discusses Music, Marriage, and His Work on Behalf of Our Armed Forces," November 6, 2011.
11. Ibid.

Chapter 2: Down, But Not Out
1. Matt Soergel, *The Florida Times Union,* "Wounded Warrior Project Message: You're Not Alone: Group Helping Injured Veterans Has Thrived Since Moving to Jacksonville," November 10, 2011.
2. Wounded Warrior Project, "Soldier Ride." https://www.woundedwarriorproject.org/programs/soldier-ride.aspx
3. Wounded Warrior Project, "TRACK." http://www.woundedwarriorproject.org/programs/track.aspx
4. Matt Soergel, *The Florida Times Union,* "Wounded Warrior Project Message: You're Not Alone: Group Helping Injured Veterans Has Thrived Since Moving to Jacksonville," November 10, 2011.
5. John H. Ostdick, *Success,* "Soldiering On: A Career Military Officer Who Lost Both Legs in Iraq Faces His Biggest Challenge: Rebuilding Other Vets' Lives," June 2012.
6. Ibid.
7. Ibid.
8. Ibid.
9. Ibid.
10. William Browning, *The Florida Times Union,* "Help for Homeless Veterans: Numbers Improving Some, but City Still Focusing on Problem," January 13, 2013.
11. Ibid.

Chapter 3: The Wounds You Can't See
1. Kristen Hannum, *U.S. Catholic,* "Nobody Knows the Trouble I've Seen," November 2012, Volume 77, Issue 11, p. 18.
2. Ibid.
3. Ibid., p. 19.
4. Robert M. Poole, *Smithsonian,* "Pathway Home," September 2010, Volume 41, Issue 5.
5. Ibid.
6. Ibid.
7. Reed McManus, *Sierra,* "A Missing Peace," July/August 2011, Volume 96, Issue 4, p. 53.
8. Ibid., p. 54.
9. Ibid.
10. Ibid
11. *USA Today,* "More Time Off Needed for Soldiers," February 1, 2011.

Chapter 4: Starting Over
1. John Donvan, NPR, *Talk of the Nation,* "Soldiers Say It's Hard To Return To Civilian Life," October 10, 2011. http://www.npr.org/2011/10/10/141213271/soldiers-say-its-hard-to-return-to-civilian-life
2. Ibid.

CHAPTER NOTES

3. Ibid.

4. Alexandra Hemmerly-Brown, *Soldiers Magazine*, "From Combat to Classroom," September 2010, p. 9.

5. Ibid.

6. Ibid.

7. Ibid. p. 11.

8. Vimal Patel, *The Eagle*, "More Veterans Seeking College Educations," February 5, 2012.

9. Ibid.

10. *The Ledger*, "Tuition Rule: Fairness in Veteran Education," January 22, 2013.

Chapter 5: You're Hired!

1. Michelle Dunlop, *The Herald (Everett, WA)*, "Tough Market for Veterans," November 11, 2011.

2. Ibid.

3. James B. Reed, *State Legislatures*, "GI Jobs," July/August 2013, Volume 39, Issue 7, p. 42.

4. Ibid., p. 43.

5. Ibid.

6. Lorri Freifeld, *Training*, "Warriors to Workers," September/October 2010, Volume 47, Issue 5.

7. Ibid.

8. *Snips*, "A Change of Duty: Program Offers Returning Soldiers New Careers," July 2013.

9. Ibid.

10. Rich Scinto, *New Haven Register*, "Foundation Outfits Veterans for Job Interviews," July 6, 2012.

11. Ibid.

FURTHER READING

Books

Canfield, Jack, et al. *Chicken Soup for the Veteran's Soul*. Deerfield Beach, FL: Health Communications, Inc., 2001.

Lewis, Kevin M. *Veterans' Voices: Personal Reflections on the Freedom Wars and Beyond*. Alexandria, VA: Vision Spots Publishing, 2013.

Montalván, Luis Carlos, and Bret Witter. *Until Tuesday: A Wounded Warrior and the Golden Retriever Who Saved Him*. New York: Hyperion, 2012.

On the Internet

Student Veterans of America
http://www.studentveterans.org/

United Service Organizations
http://www.uso.org/

Wounded Warrior Project
http://www.woundedwarrior project.org/

Works Consulted

Abele, Robert. "Gary Sinise: The Actor-Activist Discusses Music, Marriage, and His Work on Behalf of Our Armed Forces." *Idaho State Journal*, November 6, 2011.

Abrams, Michael, Michael Faulkner, and Andrea Nierenberg. *Networking for Veterans*. Boston, MA: Pearson Learning Solutions, 2013.

Browning, William. "Help for Homeless Veterans: Numbers Improving Some, but City Still Focusing on Problem." *The Florida Times Union*, January 13, 2013.

Donvan, John. "Soldiers Say It's Hard To Return To Civilian Life." NPR, *Talk of the Nation*, October 10, 2011. http://www.npr.org/2011/10/10/141213271/soldiers-say-its-hard-to-return-to-civilian-life

FURTHER READING

Dunlop, Michelle. "Tough Market for Veterans." *The Herald (Everett, WA)*, November 11, 2011.

Fagan, Kevin. "Returning Soldiers Need More Help Sooner." *San Francisco Chronicle*, November 30, 2009.

Freifeld, Lorri. "Warriors to Workers." *Training*, September/October 2010, Volume 47, Issue 5.

Gary Sinise & the Lt. Dan Band. "About the Band." http://archive.ltdanband.com/pages/about.html

Hannum, Kristen. "Nobody Knows the Trouble I've Seen." *U.S. Catholic,* November 2012, Volume 77, Issue 11.

Hemmerly-Brown, Alexandra. "From Combat to Classroom." *Soldiers Magazine*, September 2010, p. 9.

Hoge, Charles W. *Once A Warrior Always A Warrior*. Guilford, CT: Globe Pequot Press, 2010.

Klink, Stephen C. "Sunglasses." In *Chicken Soup for the Veteran's Soul,* edited by Jack Canfield, Mark Victor, and Sidney R. Slagter. Deerfield Beach, FL: Health Communications, Inc., 2001.

The Ledger, "Tuition Rule: Fairness in Veteran Education," January 22, 2013.

McManus, Reed. "A Missing Peace." *Sierra,* July/August 2011, Volume 96, Issue 4.

Ostdick, John H. "Soldiering On: A Career Military Officer Who Lost Both Legs in Iraq Faces His Biggest Challenge: Rebuilding Other Vets' Lives." *Success,* June 2012.

Patel, Vimal. "More Veterans Seeking College Educations." *The Eagle*, February 5, 2012.

Poole, Robert M. "Pathway Home." *Smithsonian*, September 2010, Volume 41, Issue 5.

Reed, James B. "GI Jobs." *State Legislatures*, July/August 2013, Volume 39, Issue 7, p. 42.

Scinto, Rich. "Foundation Outfits Veterans for Job Interviews." *New Haven Register,* July 6, 2012.

Snips. "A Change of Duty: Program Offers Returning Soldiers New Careers." July 2013.

Soergel, Matt. "Wounded Warrior Project Message: You're Not Alone: Group Helping Injured Veterans Has Thrived Since Moving to Jacksonville." *The Florida Times Union*, November 10, 2011.

Tick, Edward. *War and the Soul*. Wheaton, IL: Quest Books, 2005.

Trainor, Tim. "Heroic Firefight With Taliban Forever Changes Butte Soldier's Life." *Billings Gazette*, June 24, 2012.

USA Today. "More Time Off Needed for Soldiers." February 1, 2011.

Wilson, Kevin. "Some Normalcy Returning for Injured Soldier." *Clovis News Journal*, June 16, 2012.

Wounded Warrior Project. "Soldier Ride." https://www.woundedwarriorproject.org/programs/soldier-ride.aspx

Wounded Warrior Project. "TRACK." http://www.woundedwarriorproject.org/programs/track.aspx

GLOSSARY

amputate (AM-pyoo-teyt) — To cut off a limb (or part of a limb) through surgery.

apprentice (uh-PREN-tis) — A person who works for another in order to learn a trade.

deploy (dih-PLOI) — To send military troops to a particular area.

economy (ih-KON-uh-mee) — The management and production of resources of a community.

garrison (GAR-uh-suhn) — A body of troops stationed in a secure place.

hyper-vigilant (HAHY-per VIJ-uh-luhnt) — Excessively watchful and alert to detect danger.

lobby (LOB-ee) — To try to influence the votes of a legislative body.

post-traumatic stress disorder (pohst-truh-MAT-ik STRES dis-AWR-der) — An anxiety disorder that can occur after severe emotional trauma.

prestigious (pre-STIJ-uhs) — Having a high reputation, esteemed.

prosthesis (pros-THEE-sis) — A device that substitutes for a missing body part.

Purple Heart — A medal awarded to troops who sustained injuries in action against an enemy while serving in the US Armed Forces.

rappel (ra-PEL) — To move down a steep incline using a rope attached at the top of the incline and placed around the body.

self-sufficient (SELF-suh-FISH-uhnt) — Able to care for oneself without help.

toll (TOHL) — The loss, damage, or suffering that results from an event or action.

INDEX

ABOUT THE AUTHOR

Tammy Gagne is the author of numerous books for adults and children, including *Life on the Reservations* and *Your Guide to Becoming a US Citizen* for Mitchell Lane Publishers. She resides in northern New England with her husband and son. One of her favorite pastimes is visiting schools to speak to kids about the writing process.